RHYMECOLOGY

The Art of Hip-Hop Lyrics

RHYMECOLOGY

The Art of Hip-Hop Lyrics

JEFFREY T. WALKER, M.A.

Walker Works Publishing

Rhymecology: The Art of Hip-Hop Lyrics

Author Jeffrey T. Walker

Published by Walker Works Publishing

www.walkerworks.net

Jeffrey T. Walker is a Writer Member of ASCAP, USA

Cover Design by Gilli Moon

Edited by Karen Borger

Rhymecology Logo by Matt Ansoorian

Back over Shadow Of Hand With Microphone Photo © Kentannenbaum | Dreamstime.com

This book is available at quantity discounts for bulk purchases, for information contact the publisher above.

Printed in the United States of America

10 9 8 7 6 5 4 3 2 1

ISBN-13: 978-1518872174   ISBN-10: 1518872174 (CreateSpace Paperback version)

WHAT THEY SAY ABOUT RHYMECOLOGY AND JEFF WALKER

"Rhymecology is hip-hop as therapy. Hip-hop as healing. It is hip-hop beyond entertainment. It is hip-hop that you can actually grow and develop from."

KRS-One (Hip-hop Legend/Professor/Author)

"I have worked with and been around everyone in the entertainment industry for decades. When it comes to putting words together in a crafty, creative way, nobody does it better than Jeff Walker, nobody."

Pat O'Brien, Radio and Television Personality (CBS Sports, The Insider, Access Hollywood)

"Rhymecology represents everything that mainstream rap is not! Influenced by artists like Masta Ace and Big L, Mr. Walker keeps the tradition of lyricism alive for a new generation."

Sebastein Elkouby, Hip-Hop Publicist, Writer and Culture Specialist.

Rhymecology is a master lyricist's recipe—quite practical in many ways—for redirecting our words to the places that help, a service that great popular music has always granted."

Thomas Harrison, Ph.D. (UCLA Professor)

"Rhymecology is something all hip-hop heads should get with. It stays true to our art form while helping people. Salute!"

DJ Premier (Hip-hop Legend)

"Of all the characters I've come across in my 10 year recording career, Jeff Walker is the most wholeheartedly dedicated to raising awareness about the side of Hip Hop & Rap music that mainstream media rarely acknowledges. His writings on the complexity of rap lyrics with regard to content, and syllabic and rhythmic structure are a must for the mc/songwriter in training."
Louis Logic (Emcee, Hip-hop Historian)

"Jeff Walker can flip a rhyme as sickly as any commercial rapper. Yet he holds himself to a higher standard...This ain't some pop-culture fantasy! This is real stuff here. Anyone can tell a story. The trick is, who can elevate his / her game to ART.

Bob Bryan, Multi-Award Winning Filmmaker and creator of the Hip-Hop Documentary series, GRAFFITI VERITE

"I only knew Jeff Walker from his wet jump shot on the court. Little did I know that his 'soul' extended beyond his crossover. After listening to his spoken word, I was more than impressed as well as intrigued. In a market inundated with wannabe rap artists just trying to make a buck and 'get some tail', Jeff Walker really spoke to me. Honest, insightful, clever, humorous, real, from the heart."

Taye Diggs, Actor (Brown Sugar, How Stella got her Groove Back)

This book is dedicated to you.

ACKNOWLEDGMENTS

I offer a huge thank you to my wonderfully artistic, supportive and accomplished wife Gilli Moon. If there were more people like you, this world would be much more colorful, creative and productive.

Sincere much thanks goes to the artists who continue to make meaningful music with creatively conscious messages. Without you this book would be a lot thinner.

Thank you to my good friend Ali Kassahun. We began writing rhymes together in 1997 and have been talking hip-hop shop ever since. If I didn't have you to talk to you about multi-syllabic rhyming, I wouldn't have had anyone and this book would have never happened.

Lastly yet mostly, thank you to my parents for always allowing me to follow my passion. Your guidance and love made me who I am.

CONTENTS

The Art of Hip-Hop Lyrics

Before people were writing on phones

before we wrote hooks while designing our poems

we had pads and notebooks you could find in our homes,

These are seeds of fertile minds

that believe in internal rhymes

It's like there's an animal feeding these journal lines,

Sprouting since Magic and Bird's day

we focus on storytelling and word play,

In some genres, the lines are average

but in hip-hop the rhymes are magic

so often their poppin' cuz they're multi-syllabic,

They help you understand where some are coming from

and the intricacy of songs can be stunning some,

But peep it, we kept the secret

Close to our waist like a cummerbund

And plus, just trust,

We wouldn't tell you to do it if it wasn't fun!

Jeffrey T. Walker & Ali Kassahun

INTRODUCTION

Great lyricists tell stories. Great lyricists make us feel and relate to their point of view by painting pictures with their words. Great hip-hop lyricists are always writers but they are not always rappers. They are wordsmiths who chose hip-hop has the medium to express their creativity. There will always be a place for people who can write, whether it is in music, books or movies.

This book focuses on the art of rhyming and creating original hip-hop lyrics but its techniques can be used in any genre. It serves beginners who have never recorded a song, as well being as a handbook for experienced emcees and lyricists to "take their skills to the next level". We will cover ways to expand song-writing topics as well as revealing the intricacies behind many verses and describing what makes for classic hip-hop. Most importantly we'll push the envelope of your hip-hop thoughts so that you will create songs that resonate with and are respected by listeners of all kinds.

In order to get the most out of this book , you will need to work with it. This requires interaction with each chapter topic, the researching of songs and verses I analyze, repeatedly practicing techniques and most importantly dynamic listening. You will be asked to actively and critically listen to artists mentioned. While there is an abundant note section in the back, I recommend dedicating a new notebook to the exercises and techniques you will be learning throughout this book.

The aim of this book is not to solely make you a rapper. Instead I hope to make you an emcee with the developed skills of a great writer.

The TOPICS AND BRAINSTORMING Chapter

Hip-hop lyrics are often complex, multi-syllabic, filled with metaphors and are best used when they are included in songs that are easy to relate to and which touch the listener's emotions. While hip-hop is often generalized as being "hardcore", many of the long lasting songs, which are considered "classic", came from and continue to be creative, honest and emotional topics.

> *The key is to write songs around ideas and thoughts that you are passionate about.*

Conceiving an idea a hip-hop song is no different from any other genre. How do we come up with these elusive topics?

Don't focus on song concepts that you "should," write about. Don't feel the need to replicate current, popular song concepts. *The key is to write songs around ideas and thoughts that you are passionate about.* It doesn't matter if it's politics or peanut butter; start writing about your passion! I suppose Mr. Shawn Carter (aka Jigga, aka Hova aka Jay-Z) is passionate about money making, because has made a career off of reiterating how wealthy he is. Krs-One has lasted decades in this game while *edutaining* (entertaining + educating) us. While artists lesser known artists like Elzhi and Mickey Factz have always focused on their rhyme patterns and creative concepts that nobody has done before. They key is, each artist writes to their passion. Can you imagine Jay-Z writing a song about the health concerns with eating beef? Or Krs-One bragging about having a suite at the Trump Towers? (I'm laughing out loud imagining this).

The question is, what are you that passionate about?

Following are some ideas to get you kick started.

a) **Life experiences**. Think back on incidents that have INSPIRED you. Perhaps it was listening to someone speak or perform, maybe it was a place where you vacationed, or even watching a game. If there is one thing that lit a fire in your passion sector, that's what you should tell world about. This could also be something negative you saw/experienced that inspired you to act or live a certain way.

b) **Dreams.** Often your passion revolves around something you are striving for. Maybe you desire to be the best emcee in your school, or on your block or in the world. Okay, but tell the audience why? Perhaps you dream of money and fame. Okay, why? How would you inspire the listener to also want those things?

c) **Relationships.** Few things in life spark your passion and deep emotion in the same way that relationships do. Perhaps you have a lover who is the "air you breathe". Maybe one of your parents stuck by you through good and bad, thick and thin. A friend might have stabbed you in the back. Listeners can relate to personal stories…MAKE THEM FEEL!

d) **Message.** Your idea may be a message that you passionately wish to deliver to listeners. Maybe you want the world to be more "green". You might have a burning desire to support the idea for the re-vamping of the school system. Maybe you want to send a message about the importance of parenting. Whatever it is, tell the audience in descriptive terms so you can inspire them. But hip-hop heads don't like to be preached to! Definitely don't preach but if you deliver your message well you will light a fire in their hearts and minds!

Passion is the key to creativity. We have all seen artists, athletes and 9-5 workers who just go through the motions at some time in their career. The creativity has dried up because the passion has dried up and often the passion dries up because people don't take time to make that passion a priority. Deep stuff huh? Well we are just working on songwriting here, we will worry about life stuff later.

Now ask, yourself, does your passion fall into any of the above categories? <u>What are you passionate about?</u>

RHYMECOLOGY EXERCISE

Write a list or notes on all of the feelings, ideas, concepts and emotions that you have been passionate about in your life. This document will become a useful resource to go back to as you follow the exercises in this book..

(This is where you either go to the back of the book or begin to use your Rhymecology Notebook)

It should start something like this

I have always been passionate about…

(Remember to describe "why" this passion is so strong).

My example:

I have always been passionate about complex rhyme schemes and crafty wordplay. I love the way the rhyme patterns form a puzzle that not all minds can put together. I love being one of the ones who gets it. I am so grateful when I hear a line that makes me rewind it because there are two or three layers to the meaning.

Or it could be a list at first.

Life Passions:

Shoes, flowers, crystals, typography, aged cheese, tupperware….

The SHOW AND TELL Chapter

Whether they know it or not, most people are able to put two words together and make a rhyme. (Just think of the word "Blue", "Shoe" "Two" etc). However, to be a good lyricist you need to make people *feel*. You must inspire people to *relate*. You have to take listeners on a journey. The best rappers are writers and storytellers.

Ghostface Killah's song "All That I Got Is You" touched millions of people. The song is about him growing up poor, and the bond that is created with his mother through hardship and circumstances. There have been countless rap songs created around poverty but Ghostface used his unique choice of words to paint a distinct and unforgettable picture for us. If you were to write about being broke, how would you make us feel and relate to your personal story. Ghostface achieved this beautifully in the following lines:

> *"Seven o'clock, plucking roaches out the cereal box"*

> *"Rocking each other's pants to school wasn't easy"*

> *"But I remember this, Moms would lick her fingertips, to wipe the cold out my eye before school with her spit"*

"Mommy where's the toilet paper? 'Use the newspaper'"

These lyrics combined with a touching video and beautiful piano melody caused even the toughest guys to cry. *Ghostface* made people **feel his despair and the bond with his mother,** which reminded so many listeners of their own hard childhood. Instead of simply telling us, Ghostface **showed** us. It would have been easy to state that he *"grew up poor"* but he was more effective painting the picture of pulling *"roaches out of the cereal box"*. Instead of just telling us that his mother was there for him, he showed us by describing her *"wiping the cold out my eye with her spit"*.

This song is about Life Experiences, Dreams, Relationships and Messages (as discussed in Chapter 1). Ultimately it doesn't matter if you live in Beverly Hills or Brooklyn, this powerful song took us on a fluid, descriptive journey and immediately became a hip-hop classic.

Don't just tell listeners....

Describe...

Explain...

When you are writing or rapping, don't just *tell* listeners that you love your mother. *Describe* your mother and her actions of care and devotion in a way that will make them fall in love with her too.

Don't just *tell* listeners that you hate your old girlfriend for cheating on you; *explain* it to them in a way that is so vivid that they feel disdain and hatred for her as much as you did. Well, almost as much anyway.

We are writers. We are artists. We are storytellers. To consider ourselves simply rappers or emcees is underselling our purpose in life. We have an amazing platform where we use our words and microphones to reach out and touch people. Don't waste the opportunity!

RHYMECOLOGY EXERCISE:

Think about something (a person, item, feeling, memory) you really LOVE. Now think about something you really HATE. What brings a smile to your face? What makes you angry? What are the first things that immediately come to mind? Write them down.

I love

_____

I hate

_____

I'm inspired by

_____

I dream of

_____

Now add notes on why you love or hate that particular thing or person. It is imperative to write down <u>how</u> those things make you FEEL. Consider feeling , which others will easily relate to. <u>Why</u> does that FEELING affect you so much? <u>What</u> is the importance of that thing in your life? <u>Where</u> do you usually experience that thing?

_____

_____

_____

_____

I start to think, and then I sink Into the paper...like I was ink. When I'm writing I'm trapped in between the lines, I escape when I finish the rhyme... I got soul.

Rakim, "I Know I Got Soul", Paid in Full, 1987

The LOVE QUEST Chapter

There is one topic, which resonates with listeners of all genres of music. This one topic has been consistently present since the beginning of song writing. From *Billie Holiday,* to *The Beatles,* to *B.B. King* to *Bon Jovi*, love songs have spanned genres and generations and will continue to do so.

Yes, we are emcees and rappers but never discount the power of writing about love. You don't have to be IN love to write a great song ABOUT love. Three of the most popular ways people write about love are:

      a) The search for love

      b) The feeling of love

      c) The loss of love

Most people want to be in love, are in love, or are lamenting over the loss of love. In fact, these three feelings often consume their lives. When something is consuming your very being you search out for things that resonate with this emotional state. These things can be friends who lend an ear (just eavesdrop at your local café and you'll hear all three of these topics), books, movies and songs.

The search or desire for love can be found in "I Need Love" by L.L. Cool J.

> *"I can't believe that I found/a desire for true love*
>
> *floating around/inside my soul cuz my soul is cold/*
>
> *half of me deserves to be this way till I'm old/but the*
>
> *other half needs affection and joy/and the warmth*
>
> *created by a girl and a boy/ I need love".*

Here is one of the most popular rappers of the 1980s who was known for his crushing beats and aggressive delivery, slowing it down showing a vulnerable side. How do you think it affected his female fans? The sentiment of this song still resonates today.

On a personal note, I can testify to the metaphysical strength behind writing about the desire for love. I am happily married to an amazing, singer-songwriter named Gilli Moon. We have put out albums together and performed on each other's individual albums. Gilli is an Australian, who was born in Italy and lived in Rome…Hold up STOP! And rewind the tape to 1998! I was sitting in my college apartment with a Tascam Four-Track, some instrumentals and a notebook. I penned these lyrics about what I wanted in a woman:

> *"I want my magic rug to drop me in the middle of*

Italy/so I can see Rome and maybe find a wife/sick of being alone man damn this life/This is a love rhapsody/and one day she'll be on the cover of my rap cd/sending spiritual messages/like there's more to life than the physical and Lexuses/cuz the chest can be so appealing to me/but your mental state is much more revealing to me".

I had forgotten completely about this song until I stumbled across an old bag of cassette tapes a few years ago (after being married for 5 years). I was stunned to hear how many things had manifested from that song. My dusty four-track tape is not an example of commercial success arising from the desire for a love song, but it is an example of the more important kind of success, life success!

Hip-hop has less "pure love" songs than any other popular genre. Within the male dominated, misogynistic, and chauvinistic culture of hip-hop, it stands to reason that the rappers aim to maintain their "tough guy image". However there are still plenty of artists who do write and record love songs, and are often these are the songs that they are remembered for. Common (Common Sense at the time) was an underground emcee whose wordplay was next level. He was known in hip-hop circles and appreciated especially by those who loved intricate lyrics (like me). But it wasn't until the love song "The Light" that he was noticed by the mainstream.

Method Man was an unpredictable, raw and hungry Wu-Tang Clan emcee. While his legend may be great in the hip-hop community, his "hit songs" are few. His biggest and longest lasting "hit" is arguably one of the best rap love songs ever made. "All I Need" featuring Mary J. Blige has lines that stick in the heads of a whole generation.

> *"You don't need a ring to be wife"*
> *"Living in the lap of luxury/I'm realizing you didn't have to f*%! with me"*

> *"Back when I was nothing you made a brother feel like he was something/That's why I'm with you to this day, boo, no frontin' ".*

> *"Even when the skies were grey/you'd rub me on my back and say baby it will be okay".*

Unlike the LL Cool J song which some considered to be "soft", the Method Man song rang true to the hardcore hip-hop heads, not easy to do with a love song. The fact that this song has stood the test of time (unlike his other singles and solo album) proves the point of this chapter. Loves sells.

Love songs appeal to you when you are in love. If you are down in the dumps, the heartbreak songs will appeal to you. The hardcore, political, intellectual, gangsta emcee Immortal Technique has three albums, yet only one song about love. However, it is a gem. "You

Never Know" chronicles his relationship with a young woman. He explains how she was different than all the other girls in his hood. How they talked for hours and hours and how she made him change his 'hood ways. The story does not have a happy ending but the way it was written is enough to make any listener shed tears. It is one of three hip-hop songs that I can remember crying to. The power writers' hold in our pens, is unparalleled.

Telling a story about the 'pick up' is another powerful way to engage a listener. A classic song with this angle is by Eric B. & Rakim called "What's On Your Mind".

Rakim is best known for taking hip-hop to a superlative lyrical level in the start of the 'Golden Age'. The beats were deep and frenetic and his lyrics remain unmatched (more detail in later chapters). With this 1992 track Rakim changed it up by spitting his hood game over a mellow beat, rapping to a girl while riding in a subway car.

> *"I seen her on the subway on my way to Brooklyn,*
> *'Hello good lookin, is this seat tookin?'*
> *On the A-train, picking at her brain/*
> *I couldn't get her number, I couldn't get her name."*

It isn't an instant love connection, but we know how this subway story pans out, and ultimately Rakim's wordplay is enough to break anyone down.

RHYMECOLOGY EXERCISE:

We are exploring the search for love, the feeling of love and the loss of love.

1)Start out by choosing one state of love , which you know most about.

2) Write down all the phrases/lines that you relate with it.

3)Write down your feelings without analyzing them.

For example: Why did she leave me? Will I ever find someone else as good? I am depressed. Damn her! I miss her so bad! Who does she think she is? Life is meaningless without her. I HATE her. I still love her.

Or like so:

Silk. Chanel perfume. Salty ocean waves. Broken heart. Marvin Gaye. Burnt toast. Tears. Poetry. Sweaty socks.

The next step is to get more creative with those specific senses. Brainstorm over each. How can describe the above in a creative manner? Can you paint a picture with your words?

Do you just "miss the smell of her perfume" OR do you want to dive head first, mouth open into a swimming pool of her perfume so you can keep her scent inside you? Is your "heart just broken" OR has it been cut out of your chest with a rusty butterknife and then dropped on a bed of hot coals? Does Marvin Gaye just "remind" you of her OR would you contemplate a life in purgatory just so you could ask Marvin Gaye what inspired him to write a song that paralleled exactly how you felt about her? Did you just "cry a lot" OR did you use your tears to fill dishwashers and washing machines?

There is a distinct difference between showing and telling. Who would have thought that the advice you got from your 5th grade English teacher would be helping you with your career as a hip-hop artist?

Of course, the search, loss and feeling of love are not the only possible ways for you to write about this topic.

a) **Sex.** It is a constant subject in hip-hop and always has been. There are a plethora of rap songs created which disrespect and denigrate women, bragging about the number of sexual partners an emcee has had. Yes, it is possible that you could go that route, but why become another face in the crowd? This has been done a thousand times over. If you want to talk sex, be creative with it! See "Mind Sex" by Dead Prez or "I Get the Job Done" by Big Daddy Kane or "Still not a Player" by Big Pun.

b) **The Pick Up.** The art of the pick-up is always a fun activity to explore. The nerves. The flirtatious lines. The boasting confidence. The back and forth between a man and woman. Find a way that can bring the listener back

c) to the "crush" feelings we all had in high school. See "I Gotta Man" by Positive K, "Ms. Fat Booty" by Mos Def and "Café Girl" by Sage Francis.

d) **Story Time.** Create an engaging story for the listener so they become emotionally invested in your love story. Three verses with a beginning middle and end. See "Renee" by The Lost Boyz, "What's On Your Mind" by Eric B. and Rakim and "Brooklyn Masala" by Masta Ace.

Also you may reminisce about a lost love, the first time you fell in love, the *feeling* of cheating or being cheated on, or your philosophy of love.

<u>Please listen to and read the lyrics of these 10 love songs:</u>

"I Need Love"- L.L. Cool J

"You Never Know"- Immortal Technique

"The Light"- Common feat Mary J. Blige

"All I Need"- Method Man feat. Mary J. Blige

"You Got Me"- The Roots feat Erykah Badu

"So Into You"- Fabolous

"What's On Your Mind"- Eric B & Rakim

"Love the Way"- Murs & 9th Wonder

"Best I Ever Had"- Drake

"Renee"- The Lost Boyz

The ALPHABET & T-GRAPH Chapter

Most exceptional lyricists are constantly form words and stories in their head. Everywhere they look, they find a rhyme just waiting to be formed. They look at billboards on the freeway (can you tell I live in Los Angeles?), advertisements in magazines and even movie titles. Anywhere words are visually featured there will be words that arise in your head that rhyme with them. The featured words should become catalysts to a rhyme, which could be a catalyst to a verse, which could be a catalyst to a song.

Are you one of those lyricists who spend days and nights looking for that perfect word or phrase? Yes? No? Not sure? Don't worry because you can still create songs! The question is if don't have that knack, how can you become better with your rhymes?

A simple yet effective technique is to

USE THE ALPHABET!

From middle school students writing their first poems to seasoned emcees, the **alphabet is your best friend** when you are trying to find that perfect rhyme.

Quick, what rhymes with "trees"? Wait; really think about it...

> *A simple yet effective technique is to use the alphabet!*

wait…think…wait…now, write down your ideas… okay? How many words did you come up with? "'Trees'" is an easy word to rhyme with, and chances are that you thought of four or five right off the bat. The issue is those four or five that immediately come to mind are very likely the same words other songwriters think of. So, how can you be unique and think of more rhymes and possibly more distinct ones?

Write the alphabet on top of your page. Really do it.

A B C D E F G H I J K L M N O P Q U R S T W X Y Z

Now take your word "Trees" and go through every letter, replacing the "T" with the respective letter to see if there is a word that rhymes with it that you did not think of.

Breeze/Bees/C's/D's/Ease/Freeze/Fees/Fleas/Geez/Keys/Knees/Peas/ Please/Squease/Seas/Steez/Tease…the list goes on and on.

Note this is only rhyming single syllable words with "Trees". The list will double and triple syllable words like "Louise" or "Release". You can also select words that are not "perfect" rhymes but would easily work like "Speed" or "Deeds".

If you don't have the alphabet in front of you, just look at the letters on a keyboard computer keyboard. If I don't have either of those, do as I do and look at letters around you. They may be on an earlier page in your notebook, it could be one a poster or even on an orange juice

bottle. The source doesn't matter. Just look at the letters and let your mind run freely through every possible rhyme.

RHYMECOLOGY: T-GRAPH TECHNIQUE:

"Trees" is a one-syllable word. But we you are not reading this book just for help on one syllable word rhymes, are you? Two syllable words or "compound" rhymes are much sweeter to the ear and still not that difficult to come up with. Quick, what can you think of that rhymes with "Airplane"?

Wait….think on it….wait…WRITE…think….really? That is all you got?

Airplane is a one word made up of two single syllable words, "Air" and "Plane". To create a perfect compound rhyme you will have to rhyme with both words, perfectly. Key here is the fact you don't have to chose one word to rhyme. It could be two words such as "Dare" and "Jane". In a sentence you could write,

"I dared Jane to jump off the airplane".

Both "Air" and "Plane" are simple one syllable words but yet why is it so difficult to come up with s number of matching phrases right off the bat? Here is where we can use the Rhymecology T-Graph Technique. You will use the alphabet just as you did for the "Trees" rhyme scheme. You are going to do that with both "Air" and "Plane"

separately. This is important. Do NOT try to rhyme both words together. Individually rhyme with each.

Create your T-Graph by writing each word on the same line, spaced out, underlined and divided by another line. Huh? Yeah…just look below.

Air	Plane
Stare	Grain
Fair	Brain
Share	Name
Pear	Main
Wear	Lame
Tear	Stain

(there are dozens more but let's move on)

"Stare Grain? "Pear Main"? Those make no sense! Worry not.

The next step is taking the word "pear" and connecting it with each of the words underneath "Plane".

Pear Grain

Pear Brain

Pear Name

Pear Main

Pear Lame

Pear Stain

Not many of the combinations make very good sense here. But how about Pear Stain? This is not something that you would normally have thought of right off the bat in regards to rhyming with "Airplane". But all of a sudden you have "I Dared Jane to sit next to that lady with the pear stain on the airplane". Getting richer isn't it?

Look back at the list and let's do the same thing with the word "Share". Go down the list and see what matches with it.

Share Grain

Share Brain

Share Name

Share Main

Share Lame

Share Stain

A few more options here already. Do you see how this technique brings out word combinations that you might not have thought in your regular rhyming technique? Now you have 4 combinations, giving off 8 rhymes.

Pear + Share + Dared + Air = 4.

Stains + Grains + Jane + Plane=4.

"How can you complain about wine and pear stains/when I'm so broke I have to share grains/with my neighbor who just dared Jane to jump out of an airplane".

Now do the same thing with the word "Bedroom". Divide the word into two. Write down the word "Bed" and the word "Room" and just match them up one at a time!

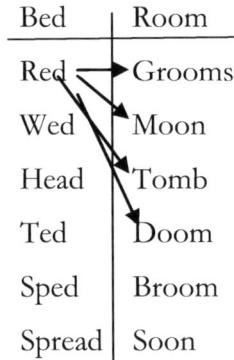

Bed	Room
Red	Grooms
Wed	Moon
Head	Tomb
Ted	Doom
Sped	Broom
Spread	Soon

Take the first word, "Red" and match it with all the possible rhymes underneath "Room". You will notice many possible combinations (always easier with colors and nouns).

Red Groom

Red Moon

Red Tomb

Red Doom

Red Broom

Red Soon

Using your Rhymecology notebook, continue matching each of the "bed" rhymes with each of the "room" rhymes in the same manner as shown above. Combinations don't always have to make sense, just practice making the match!

I saw promise in the combinations of "Wed Grooms", "Head Tombs", "Ted's Broom", "Red Moon", "Red Wombs", "Said Whom", "Meds Loom". Between bedroom, wed grooms, red wombs and all the rest you could probably come up with some kind of story about a Ted's wedding and a then a fight with a broom where someone had to go to the hospital…actually let me just write a quick verse to show you what I am thinking .

"It was a cold night with fog and a red moon

but it was hot inside of the couple's bedroom

until Barb ran to the closet and grabbed Ted's broom

yelled out "pick what you want on your head tomb!"

It all came about from the initial writing down of the rhymes. Then I looked at the words and asked myself, "How can I make them work together?" Does this have the possibility of becoming a story?

In basketball, when you learn to play you are taught that the backboard is your friend. If your shot hits in the painted square, chances are very high that the shot will go into the basket. As we get older, unfortunately, most of us stray away from our trusty backboard shot in hopes of the more glamorous swish. Like the backboard for basketball players, the alphabet and the T-Graph will always be there for lyricists.

RHYMECOLOGY EXERCISE:

Write down the alphabet. The twist here is I want you to write a "fancy" alphabet. Use a stencil, add color or choose a cool font on the computer. Use what you have in order to make it really fun to look at. Keep it by your desk or in your notebook so that you don't have to write a new alphabet every time you try to formulate a rhyming word or scheme.

RHYMECOLOGY EXERCISE 2:

Once you have done your alphabet, put it next to a blank page in your notebook and practice using it. Start out with one syllable words like

1) READ 2) FLOOD 3) TRAP

(Or replace these options with your preferred one-syllable words) then utilize your fancy alphabet by exploring each letter as described in the chapter. Then step it up and push it to writing down two-syllable words.

1) MIXTAPE 2) GREENDAY 3) PEACOCK

This is where you set up the T-Graph Technique. In later chapters, and as a writer you will decide on your own words, plug them in and fill out your own graphs.

The WARM UP SONG Chapter

What is your:

     a. Name and age

     b. Favorite food

     c. Favorite music

     d. Favorite things to do

     e. Who do you live with

     f. One thing you love/One thing you hate

     g. One thing that is interesting about you

Let's say that your name is **Jon,** and you are **18 years old**. Your favorite food is **Mexican food.** Favorite music is **Rap.** You like to play **video games**. You live in a **group home**. One thing you love to do is **skateboard** and one thing you hate is **school**. Something interesting is that you can hold your breath.

Write down the key words (bolded above) and some words that rhyme with them. If you have no idea what rhymes with **Jon** write down the alphabet on top of the page.

A B C D E F G H I J K L M N O P Q R S T U V W X Z Y

Replace the 'J' in Jon with each letter in the alphabet and without judgment or pause, frenetically come up with rhymes.

Bomb. Con. Gone. Kong. Long. Lawn. Pawn. Song. Strong. Wrong.

Next fill in the sentences. We have the name **Jon** and a bunch of words that rhyme with his name. A perfect first line for this is always, "My name is Jon (or whatever the name is) and this is my song!" Maybe you are on the football team, possibly a big guy. Look at the possible words above. What could you use?

"My name is Jon, this is my song/ They say I am strong as King Kong".

Maybe you are 18. So what rhymes with "teen"? Go to the alphabet.

Been. Dean. Fiend. Green. Jeans. Mean. Lean. Scene. Team. Theme.

Which word can you associate with Jon? Let's say your favorite color is "green". Maybe you like to wear Levi "Jeans".

"My name is Jon this is my song/ They say I am strong as King Kong/ Right now I'm eighteen/ at home I never make a scene cuz she can be mean..."

Let's say that you like to skateboard. I would use the verb "Skating" here and plug it in.

Baiting. Dating. Faking. Hating. Making. Rating. Taking. Waiting.

What word can you use here? Let's use "hating".

"My name is Jon this is my song/ I am strong as King Kong/ Right now I'm eighteen/ at home I never make a scene cuz she can be mean/ My favorite thing to do is skating/ It keeps me away from people that are hating…"

This is a simple rhyme technique but it shows how, in a short amount of time to devise with a half a poem/rap that is cool, creative and introspective. Sometimes your will think of rhymes quickly, other times you will literally need to write lists of words out just as you did in chapter. Eventually the process becomes a familiar mental exercise. But don't worry, it will get more complex.

"I heard you rhyme a few times,

each time you blew it.

You're soft, you can't go off, I knew it.

Let's be realistic,

I'm not egotistic;

But you, your crew…just not that artistic.

Point blank: your song stank.

I know you want the truth, so let's be frank."

-   **Chill Rob G, "Let the Words Flow," Ride the Rhythm, 1989.**

*(moral of the story, you if you don't get your rhyme skills up, you may be
the subject of a Chill Rob G diss)*

The ACTIVE LISTENING Chapter

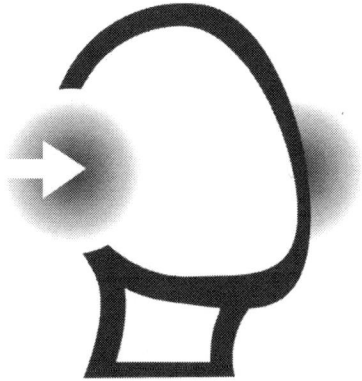

To be able to craft evocative, creative prose either on the spot, freestyle or in written form takes time. It does not happen overnight. After years of studying rhyme patterns in hip-hop, writing down rhymes and freestyling in many different situations, it becomes almost effortless to conjure up words that rhyme. To say something like *"I'm just sitting here typing/ sipping beer, writing/ sticking near, the lightning/ it's fitting, it's frightening"* sounds nice to the ear because of the fast hitting compound rhymes but that is something that I just came up with in a few seconds because I am drinking a beer in the rain under a sky crackling with lightning. So how do I create a sentence with five syllables rhyming four times in five seconds? As with any sport, endeavor or creative process, it takes practice. Practice rhyming and also practice listening!

It doesn't matter if it takes a minute, an hour, a day or a week. Seasoned emcees just don't allow themselves to settle on rhymes because they have LISTENED to themselves

> *Practice rhyming but also practice listening!*

and peers for so long, they know what is going to sound right. Just like anything, it takes practice. Practicing rhyming but also practicing listening!

When I listen to a song, I don't zoning out thinking about lunch. I remain focused. When I listen, I work. You should consider listening to be a useful exercise too. In my head I spell out the lyrics that I hear from the speakers. When I hear a rhyme, I always imagine the words on the page, and if it is a good one, I begin counting on my fingers. What I am doing is counting the syllables that the emcee rhymed between the two sentences. Peep the following Louis Logic bars:

"Jimmity Crickets

I got another cop giving me tickets

what would my life be if it didn't seem wicked

even my landlord said she'd love to see me evicted…"

What did you notice in these few lines? Did you see a rhyme scheme? How many syllables did he rhyme? Did he paint a picture in a few lines about what his life is about? Active listening. I am counting the number of syllables the emcee rhymes, looking at each word in each sentence matching it up with the words in the next sentence.

Break it down into syllables:

"Jim-me-ity-crick-ets"

"giv-en-me-tick-ets"

"did-n't-seem-wick-ed"

"see-me-evic-ted".

Notice that each of the quoted rhymes is 4/5 syllables. It is very difficult to make perfect rhymes when you get above three or four syllables. The more syllables you can rhyme together, the better it sounds to the listener and the more respected you will be by other emcees. More on this later.

To become a great emcee it is absolutely essential to become an active listener of great emcees. It is, of course, imperative to study their delivery (the way they flow) but also crucial to understand the WAY they WRITE. Too often, aspiring emcees focus on flow and existing trends and not enough on the writing! The greatest emcees are great writers and that is why they last through generations. Look at the career of someone like a Kool G. Rap or a Nas. These are artists who are evolving with the times and their writing reflects that. An artist like Tone Loc, who had a bigger individual hit ("Wild Thing") than these two artists, didn't write the majority of his lyrics and has since not been able to keep up.

One artist who is the definition of keeping up and evolving with the culture is Masta Ace. Masta Ace was a Juice Crew member (including Craig G, Kool G. Rap, and Big Daddy Kane) who was featured on the legendary posse track, "The Symphony" in 1988. He then went on to bring in the car culture with songs like "Born to Roll" and "The I.N.C. Ride". However, being the writer that he is, his writing matured as he matured. He then went on to release two of the greatest post 90's albums in *Disposable Arts* and *A Long Hot Summer*. The two albums create one incredible story. The following is a verse written by the Masta Ace on the song "Beautiful".

This is brand new Uptown, still in the box
This the Yankees 10-nothin', killin' the Sox
This ain't huggin' the block wit' a gat in ya hand
This is Boca Ratan on a Catamaran
With the sun beamin' down, where you at in the sand?
I feel like I'm more than a cat wit' a plan
This feels like it's more than a flash in the pan
This is milk in the cup and cash in ya hand
This is a warm coat on the coldest night
That's why I stole this mic, y'all don't hold this right
The first in a class of many
This is a bottle of Jack, no a glass of Henny
Now drink it up 'til there ain't nothin' left in it
I'm reppin' it, BK, that's a definite
There's more of these amazing rhymes
A song like this in these days and times… is beautiful

Masta Ace "Beautiful", A Long Hot Summer, 2004

What did you notice about his writing? What did you feel in reading or listening to the verse? Let's break this verse down, all the way down! (feel free to jot notes on the verse itself).

HOW TO STUDY A VERSE

1. Notice the rhyming patterns
2. Count the number of syllables in the rhymes
3. Go back and listen as you read over the verse
4. What feeling did you get from hearing/reading the verse?

A) In the first line Ace delivers 6 syllables (through "uptown") takes a breath and then delivers the last 4 ("still in the box") after taking a breath. In the second line Ace matches the syllables in the first line by delivering 7 syllables (until "nothing") and then finishes it out with 4 syllables ("killin' the Sox") that match the first line perfectly. 10 Syllables in the first line. 11 in the second. With the last 4 syllables of each line creating perfect rhymes, it is sweet to the ear. The next two lines are delivered with no breath, each line holding 12 syllables. Later in the verse Ace pauses before delivering "The first in a class of many" only 8 syllables and then continues straight into the next line with no breaths and delivers "this a bottle of Jack, no a glass of Henny" which is 13 syllables. If lines are mismatched by number of syllables, the second line should normally contain more than the first.

B) Notice the way that Masta Ace rhymes multiple syllables in each of the lines. "Class of many" is a perfect match for "glass of Henny". And "Coldest night" in one line is then matched two times by "stole this mic" and "hold this right". Sometimes he rhymes one word with a few words ("Gat in ya hand" with "Catamaran").

C) After you have combed over the way your artist matches syllables and rhyme patterns, then listen to the way the verse is delivered. In the verse by Masta Ace he has it all. It is written beautifully, it is delivered smoothly and patiently, it is positive and hip-hop in its true purest form!

D) After studying the lyrics and delivery, take a moment to "feel" the verse. How did Ace make you feel? What picture did he paint for the listener? "Cash in your hand", "Boca Raton on a catamaran", "Yankees 10 nothing killing the Sox," "Warm coat on the coldest night". His words are painting pictures which make the listener feel good. Who can't relate to having a warm coat on a freezing night? Who doesn't like cash in their hand? He set out to make you feel "Beautiful" and as he always does, he accomplished that.

As fans we tend to put our favorite songs or verses on a pedestal.

We feel inspired by those songs, but we rarely think that we can reach the level of accomplishment found in those favorite verses. However, when we write down the songs or verses and study them we realize that they are just words. They are words that came from an artist's mind after years of listening, studying and practicing. Are you willing to listen, study and practice? Of course you are. Your idols did the same thing that you are doing!

"Just because you are listening doesn't mean that you are *hearing!*"

~ Wesley Snipes

White Men Can't Jump.

The ART OF IMMITATION Chapter

When I was creating my first professional demo, my producer (Joey Swartz, SLAMM studios, Los Angeles) understood how I *wanted* to rhyme. At the time I could write a bunch of rhyming words, but the problem was I had no skill in rapping to the beat or getting my words down in rhythm. He gave me a metronome and told me to write down all the words to one of my favorite verses and then study it over and over again. He told me to put my verses next to the chosen verse and just notice the difference at first. After comparing the two, he told me to plug my own words into the exact rhyme scheme from verse I chose. The artist AZ on his song "Sugar Hill" wrote one of the verses I loved at the time.

> *"No more cutting grams or*
> *wrapping grands up in rubber bands*
> *I'm a recovered man,*
> *I wrote plans to discover other lands*
> *suburban places got me seeking for oasis*
> *Crystal by the cases, ladies of all races with dime faces*
> *sex on the white sand beaches of St. Thomas*
> *though this ain't promised,*
> *I'm as determined as them old timers..."*

I was actually hesitant to write it out at first, thinking that I was a "lyricist in my own right" and wondering "what good that would do". However, everyone sees different things when they write out a verse. I noticed that AZ was not too wordy. I noticed that many of his lines had rhymes within the sentence. I looked at my sentences in my notebook and they were very wordy compared to AZ. So I started to listen to other rappers I liked and noticed that they never a wasted word. I discovered that the rhythm and delivery were more important than fitting in every word. At the time I thought every lyric was vital and just *had* to be in the line, but I was cramming in too many syllables and overrunning the beat. From writing down those lyrics, came more active listening and from more active listening I developed better lyric writing skills.

There is a simple equation at work here. You get what you focus on. Even when listening to a song, you work on your craft. If you want to just chill and relax at home you have certain artists who you go to. If you are at a club wanting to get down on the dance floor, it is a different type of artist that you will be wanting to hear. But if you want to be a hip-hop lyricist, you take your Big L, your Blackaliscious, your Big Pun into your room with a pen and a pad, put on some headphones and hang a sign that says, "Do Not Disturb" on your door.

Artists used to print out their lyrics on the inside cover of their tape or CD. This makes it easy to see how they write, but my suggestion is to take one or two of the tracks and physically **copy** them out in your own writing, in your notebook. Then create your work with what you have copied as a guideline. The goal is to understand the format of the rhymes and the way that great lyricists put them together. Eventually, you'll VISUALIZE the page and SEE the lyrics being written on it at the same time as you are hearing the words come through your headphones. Once you are able to see the lyrics form, you are on your way to becoming a better rapper/emcee/freestyler/artist. It all starts with active listening.

"**When you are listening to somebody, completely, attentively, then you are listening not only to the words, but also to the feeling of what is being conveyed, to the whole of it, not part of it.**"[1]

~Jiddu Krishnamurti

RHYMECOLOGY EXERCISE:

Pick three songs of your favorite songs. Pick the verse from each song that resonates with you the most. Write down every word in your Rhymecology notebook.

Listen to the verse repeatedly (at least 10 times) as you read what you have written. Listen, listen, and listen again to the lyrics but also the pauses, the breaths.

After you feel like you really understand the message and delivery, write your own verse. Write it in a similar style, similar rhythm. For this exercise it does not matter what you say, it is just the flow and the style to show yourself what they do and what you can do.

The DON'T SETTLE ON RHYMES Chapter

When you study great verse you should notice that every word, line, rhyme and space is thought out with extreme care. There are no wasted words! A true lyricist takes their time until the right word; phrase or verse comes to them. A novice will settle for something that is "close" or "good enough".

If you are having trouble finding the perfect word or devising the optimum phrase, **step away from the page**! Oft times, after an extended writing period our brains need a break. Imagine you are trying to lift your weights one last time but your arms are shaking and you just can't do it. What do you do? You put down the weights and walk around the gym, giving yourself a break. After that you either go back with renewed energy to lift again or you maybe just come back the next day. Either way you needed to give your muscles a break! Treat your writing the same way. If you overextend yourself at the gym you may tear a muscle. If you overextend yourself in lyric writing you may ruin your song.

The alphabet check and the T-Graph technique from earlier could help you get outside of your box. If that doesn't help it could be time to outsource. We should all have a friend we can call on when we are stuck on a word or line. You can always refer to a Rhyming Dictionary. There is one by Kevin M. Mitchell called the *Hip Hop Rhyming Dictionary*. If that is too old school for you, online there is www.rhymezone.com. The absolute best rhyme assistant I have seen is the app Rhymers Block.

1.Step away from the page

2. Alphabet check & T-Graph Technique

3. Ask for help from a lyricist friend

4. Use a rhyming dictionary

5. Download Rhymers Block (app)

If you are still stuck on trying to find that perfect rhyme, take a detour! It might be time to mix up your wording. Try to put the end of the line at the beginning or the beginning at the end. What other words can you use that mean the same thing? (right click on your computer for synonyms). What other ways can you say it?

Let's pretend you are trying to tell the listener that you "My flow is hotter than lava". You really wouldn't say that because it is pretty corny. But lets say for some reason you really want to get that point across but you just can't find the perfect rhyme to go with "lava". Play around with the phrases. Change the order, change the wording, try synonyms and how else can you say it?

Try "**Like lava my flow is hot**" or "*Lava isn't as hot as my flow*" or "MY FLOWS MAKE LAVA SEEM COLD" or "I flow so hot, lava gets jealous" or even "My words can burn lava, YO!". So now instead of focusing on the obscure word "lava", you are making the same point and have the option to rhyme with "hot", "flow", "cold", "jealous" or "yo".

If none of these techniques work, you may need to scrap the whole line! I know this is hard, however if you've fallen in love with some magical metaphor and can't make the line work… scrap it! Delete it. Lava. Perhaps you'll use again in another song, but don't let it stop your progress in this one.

In the ultra-competitive world of hip-hop you cannot afford to settle on one line to make another one work. For an aspiring hip-hop artist, one weak line could be the deal breaker.

The Commonality of Common Themes:

I got a piece of advice that I'll never forgot from singer-song writer Kim Erin. My first stage name was The Poetic Prophet (probably should have kept that one). She told me to look through my songs and verses and notice how many times I said the word "prophet" or "sage". She challenged me to write a song that didn't include either word. I noticed that on the demo I said either prophet or sage 6 times on 10 songs. Way too much. I loved how "page" and "sage" went together but I was repeating myself.

We all know Tupac Shakur is one of the all-time greats. If you know Tupac you know he had certain rhymes that he fell back on often. He is one of the few legends able to do that and get away with it. He often would rhyme "*DRUG DEALER*" and "*THUG NIGGA*" (Did you notice I used font similar to the Thug Life tattoo on this belly? It's the little things, you know?) As well as "*HENNESSEY*" and "*ENEMIES*". But if you listen to the song *"Pain"*, he goes too far. The following lines are not the hook, these are in the verses. He only had two verses in the song as Birdman featured in the second verse.

Verse 1: ***I'm drinkin' Hennessey***
Runnin' from my enemies
Verse 3: ***I'm a nut and drinkin' Hennessey***
And gettin' high on tha lookout for my enemies

While we may love how well the compound rhymes match it is still no excuse for the repetition. Even if Pac is your all-time favorite, you know he could have done better than that. Moral of the story, rhyme three syllables but don't repeat the exact rhyme scheme in the very next verse you spit!

RHYMECOLOGY EXERCISE:

Look through your past notebook of rhymes (or your phone)and find common themes. This means intensely combing over your pages and songs. What words do you repeat? What themes re-appear? Is there a song in which you mention the same thing twice?

Note these themes or words on a list.

Keep these two lists handy and in your next three verses DO NOT use any of those topics and DO NOT use any of those same rhymes.

I GOT A SMILE THAT'LL MAKE THE MIRROR CRACK

AND I SEEM TO STAY UNDER CLOUDS THAT'S PITCH BLACK.

SO WHEN IT RAINS, IT POURS, AND WHEN IT POURS, I'M SOAKED.

I CONTRACTED LUNG CANCER FROM THIRD HAND SMOKE,

AND I'M LIKE THE FROG THAT'S DYING TO BE A PRINCE,

THE BOY WHO CRIED WOLF AND NO ONE WAS CONVINCED.

THE MAN WHO HIT LOTTO AND LOST HIS TICKET,

IN A RAINSTORM...AND STRUCK BY LIGHTNING TRYING TO GET IT.

- GZA, "Life Is a Movie," Pro Tools, 2008

The RAKIM Chapter

Francisco Goya is one of the greatest artists of his century (born 1748). Considered by many to be the "father of modern painting", he was the first artist to paint his subjects (often kings and queens) exactly as they looked, even if they were not pretty to look at. Let's be honest a lot of them were ugly. Artists before Goya painted their subjects in ways that falsely flattered the subjects. Goya painted realistically, truthfully. So even though many other artists were and would become more famous, most of them would not have been able to do what they did without Francisco Goya's groundbreaking techniques. Hip-hop has one artist who's impact was as dramatic as Goya's, his name is Rakim. In this chapter we will analyze how his innovative rhyme schemes paved the way for today's emcees and rappers.

I have often heard grumblings like "Oh anyone can rap…" and things of that nature. There may be some truth to that statement. In fact, it is not difficult to rhyme words like "cat" and "bat" over a slow loop (repeating beat). However, there are lots of contemporary lyricists who have taken the form to new levels. The innovators have accomplished this through intelligence and exhaustive practice, working on their craft over, and over, and over.

By comparison, a great hip-hop lyricist more than doubles the amount of rhyming that an artist from another genre performs. A celebrated hip-hop lyricist may take the same rhyme pattern and repeat it, with rhythm, for a full verse. A first class hip-hop lyricist takes that same rhyme pattern and then in the middle of the sentence may throw in another rhyme pattern without losing the original.

An example of rock lyrics would be the Smashing Pumpkins:

> *"It's almost over it's almost over*
> *No more war and no more soldiers*
> *To stand against his love*
> *Away with all the troubles that you've made*
> *Away with waiting for another day*
> *Look ma the sun is shining on me*
> *Impatient, in love and aching to be..."*

A great verse indeed. In the first line there are 10 syllables and in the second line there are 8. In the last two lines there are 9 and then 10. So we see that the spacing is well placed and there are the rhymes of *"over"* and *"soldier"* and *"made"* and *"day"* and then *"me"* and *"be"*.

"Shining on me" and *"aching to be"* is a perfect match as far as the syllables go. *"Shin-ing on me"* matches *"ach-ing to be"* with the four syllables lined up. In rock music that might be good but in the today's complex world of hip-hop lyrics, that would not cut it!

A good hip-hop lyricist not only matches the syllables perfectly but also rhymes each of the syllables perfectly. For example if I was writing the last lines, it might be something like (in different context):

> *"Look ma the sun is shining on me*
> *Impatient, as I'm climbing through trees..."*
>
> OR
>
> *"These rappers all sound crazy to me*
> *Impatient and too lazy to be..."*

A great hip-hop lyricist would not rhyme the phrases "shining on me" with "aching to be". To a hip-hop lyricist, the words "crazy to me" and "aching to be" come together like a piece of a puzzle.

Emcees who put together perfect rhyming patterns are much more common than ever before. This skill does develop overnight, however. I observe that in my classes one of the hardest things to pick up is turning ideas into rhymes. This is because this specific skill does not come naturally in the start. Most writers, lyricists and rappers starting out have their hands and heads full simply devising a good line that rhymes with the last sentence. This makes sense considering the pioneers of hip-hop (Sugar Hill Gang, Kurtis Blow, Grandmaster Flash and The Furious Five) also began with what would now be considered simplistic rhyme schemes. For example, 1979 mega hit by Sugar Hill Gang:

"Said a hip hop the hippie to the hippie

the hip hip hop, a you dont stop

the rock it to the bang bang boogie say up

jumped the boogie

to the rhythm of the boogie, the beat

skiddlee beebop a we rock a scoobie doo

and guess what america we love you

"Rappers Delight" was the first rap song to have commercial success and for that it is still one of the most important songs ever made. Of course, the rhyme schemes and patterns are simple, as most songs were at the time. From the early to mid 1980's, hip-hop was growing as a cultural phenomenon with groups like Run DMC, LL Cool J and the Beastie Boys. They are all hip-hop legends and will always be. However, LYRICAL standards changed when **Eric B. & Rakim** released *Paid in Full* in 1987. Simply, **Rakim changed the game**.

Artists such as Nas, Method Man, Tupac, 50 Cent, Eminem and more have all claimed that Rakim was the one they wanted to be like. The one who inspired them to rhyme in more complex ways. Eric B. and Rakim were described by journalist Tom Terrell of NPR as "the most influential DJ/MC combo in contemporary pop music period". They were also nominated for induction into the Rock and Roll Hall of Fame. In 2012, hip-hop magazine, *The Source* ranked Rakim #1 on their list of the "Top 50 Lyricists of All Time".

He was rapping in the 80's, he can't be all that you might be thinking. Well, before Rakim, single syllable rhymes were placed at the end of each sentence to punctuate the point. See Sucker MCs:

"Two years ago, a friend of mine

Asked me to say some MC rhymes

So I said this rhyme I'm about to say

The rhyme was Def a-then it went this way

Took a test to become an MC

And Orange Krush became amazed at me

So Larry put me inside, his Cad-illac

The chaffeur drove off and we never came back

Dave cut the record down to the bone

And now they got me rockin on the microphone

Note that the only rhyme is at the end of each line.

"Mine"-"Rhymes"

"Say"- "Way"

"MC"- "Me"

"-Lac"-"Back"

"Bone"-"-Phone"

Note that when the rhyme drops, the line stops. The thought is concluded and you have to wait for the next line to find out the next thought which Run is going to tell us. For the better part of the late 1970's and 1980's this was the norm. We were just waiting for our Goya.

Rakim not only raised the bar for lyricists, he took rhyming to such a high level of sophistication that it would take years for many other lyricists to even get close. *Paid in Full* showcased Rakim's multi-syllabic lyrical delivery which would be later adapted by numerous rappers —introducing the idea of a rapid, continuous, free-rhythmic flow, based around deeply woven rhyme structures (incorporating internal rhymes and sophisticated metaphors). Rakim's "Paid in Full":

"So I start my mission, leave my residence

Thinkin' how could I get some dead presidents

I need money, I used to be a stick-up kid

So I think of all the devious things I did

I used to roll up, this is a hold up, ain't nuthin' funny

Stop smiling, be still, don't nuthin' move but the money

But now I learned to earn 'cuz I'm righteous

I feel great, so maybe I might just

Search for a nine to five, if I strive

Then maybe I'll stay alive

So I walk up the street whistlin' this

Feelin' out of place 'cuz, man, do I miss

A pen and a paper, a stereo, a tape of

Me and Eric B, and a nice big plate of

Fish, which is my favorite dish

But without no money it's still a wish"

Doesn't seem that fancy does it? Well, hold on now. Rakim was the first to make sure that almost all of his rhymes where multi-syllabic. Rhymes such as "residence" and "presidents". Notice how the two words have two different rhyming syllables. Broken down into syllables "resi" matches "presi" while "dence" matches "dents".

Not only did he create multi-syllabic rhymes in his words, he also was able to rhyme two words with three words because of the matching syllables. This is evidenced in "plate of fish" and "favorite dish" above.

As seen in "Sucker MCs" each sentence would end in a thought or an action. As you can see in Rakim's verse, most of the lines lead into the next.. In the following line, Rakim leaves us hanging in two consecutive lines. He feels so great he might just…might just what?? Oh, search for a 9 to 5. But if he does strive at that 9 to 5…well what will happen??

I feel great, so maybe I might just
Search for a nine to five, if I strive

This is done again and again. "Man do I miss…" has got the listener hanging, wondering what Rakim misses. And again with "a nice big plate of…" has got us wondering what exactly is on that nice big plate. Is it a steak? Is it some chicken? Some rice? No no, Rakim likes his fish apparently.

Is that enough? Well, Rakim ALSO introduce internal rhyme scheme as well. After setting the stage with the rhyme "*paper*" and "*tape of*" (pronounced *tape uh*) he throws in "*me and Eric B*" before completing the previous rhyme with "*plate of*" (again pronounced *plate uh*).

A pen and a paper, a stereo, a tape of
<u>Me</u> and <u>Eric B</u>, and a nice big plate of

This is where sophistication and complexity all began. The rhyme schemes today have reached incredible levels and improve each and every year. As we leave behind those formative years of hip-hop, fewer and fewer new generations may consider Rakim to be one of the greatest. However, books, hip-hop historians and old school artists will try to keep him relevant and important because without Rakim there would be no Nas, no Jay-Z, nor Eminem.

RHYMECOLOGY EXERCISE:

Write an eight line verse with at least two multi-syllabic lines (see: hate cars + eight bars below). In the verse add one inner sentence rhyme. (Rakim's "me and *Eric b*" as example above and my "*dare to swear*" below.)

Example:

> *It doesn't matter if you love or hate cars*
> *Because it's your turn to write eight bars*
> *That make sense and rhyme emphatically*
> *You can write comically or even dramatically*
> *A <u>rhyme</u> within a <u>line</u> would be great*
> *And if you <u>dare</u> to <u>swear,</u> we're still straight*
> *You got a friend? Then it's cool to mock him*
> *Just as long as his name is not Rakim~*

BONUS: The classic, groundbreaking, Eric B. And Rakim albums include: *Paid in Full* and *Follow the Leader* and *Let the Rhythm Hit Em.* (*hint…STUDY THEM!*)

I start thinking: How many souls
hip-hop has affected? How
many dead folks this art
resurrected? How many nations
this culture connected? Who
am I to judge one's
perspective?

- Common, "6th Sense,"
Like Water for Chocolate, 2000.

The RHYME SCHEME Chapter

There are dozens of different types of rhyme schemes. Some are simple (pop music) others are more complex (underground hip-hop) but they all share the same fundamental form and principles. A rhyme scheme is the pattern of the rhymes. Rhyme schemes are not singular to musical songs, as they have been prevalent in some of the greatest literature (See Dante's <u>Divine Comedy</u> or Virgil's <u>The Aeneid</u>).

Being a hip-hop lyricist means that as the writer you are free to create almost any rhyme scheme you desire. There are no rules in place, however let's first analyze a few of the classic rhyme schemes.

Historically, in a four bar verse the third line is not required to rhyme with any word. Lots of pop songs have been written in the format of A/B/C/B.

> *Hip Hop encourages you to create original rhyme schemes and patterns*

PATTERN 1

A/B/C/B

(A) I went to the store

(B) To buy some food

(C) When I came out

(B) I was in a bad mood

This is the simplest pattern; and one used in elementary school poetry. There is nothing wrong with it. In fact the simplicity of it lends and opportunity to add **supplemental rhymes**.

I went to the store (A)

To buy (B) some fries (B)

When I came out (C)

I was high (B) and dry (B)

OR

I went to the store (A)

To buy some food (B)

But I learned (C) it burned (C)

So I was in a bad mood (B)

OR

I went to the store (A)

to buy (B) some fries (B)

But I learned(C) it burned (C)

So I was high (B) and dry(B)

As demonstrated, with the use of supplementals, even the simplest of rhyme schemes becomes more fun and engaging. Another classic yet simple scheme is one that was used in lots of early hip-hop songs.

PATTERN 2

A/A/B/B

(A) I am writing a book

(A) and it's a good look

(B) its filled with knowledge

(B) I didn't get in college

This rhyme scheme lends as a perfect place for **internal rhyme.**

I am writing a book (A)

And it's a good look (A)

I am **filled(B)** with knowledge(C)

Cuz the **ill (B)skill (B)** I got in college (B)

Or extreme internals

I'm **fighting(A) writing(A)** this book (B)

But I **heard(C)** the **words(C)** are a good look (B)

So I my **quill(D) filled(D)** it with knowledge(E)

From the **ill(D) skill (D)**I gained in college (E)

PATTERN 3

A/A/A/A

My friend gave me a call (A)

Told me meet him at the mall (A)

Instead I went to play ball (A)

With Peter, Joe and Paul (A)

With this scheme the possibilities are endless. One way to make it juicier would be to double up on the supplemental rhymes.

I got a call (A) at the mall (A)

Paul (A) wanted to play ball (A)

They asked me cuz I'm tall (A)

But I said, "No cuz ya'll (A) are too small (A)

You are saying, 'Okay but that is just rhyming one word a few times over'. True, but once you learn the basic concept you then develop the skills to build and expand upon it. There are many good rappers but one of the greatest rappers with dazzling rhyme schemes is *Fabolous*. In the following rhyme he tackles the aforementioned patterns deftly.

"My babys the only one I bring(A) to the villa(B)

that can get the bling(A) and the scrilla(B)

Girl, I know you smooth enough to spring(A) a Chinchilla(B)

and still take a sting(A) of Tequila(B),

the way you swing(A) is a thriller(B)

I'm watchin (C)that(D) like the boxing(C) match (D)

in the ring(A)of Manila(B)".

Notice how this is a remixed version of the first three patterns discussed? The reason it doesn't sound boring is because instead of merely rhyming the last syllable of the last word, he rhymes multiple syllables in multiple words. Notice, "*bring to the villa*" matches perfectly with the syllables from "*bling and the scrilla*" and "*sting of Tequila*" and so on. Adding extra words and syllables keeps an emcee from sounding monotonous, especially if they maintain the same rhyme scheme for eight or sixteen lines!

Another well-known hip-hop rhyme scheme is smashing the same rhyme scheme as many times as possible and in the same line. **It's like tripling your internals!** Big Daddy Kane was the inventor of this rhyme scheme and he did it at the time when most of the rhyme schemes were still A-A-B-B. Big Daddy Kane, along with Kool Moe Dee, is considered and acknowledged as one of the pioneering masters of *fast rap*. Here he is in "Smooth Operator" (1989):

"Confuse (1) and lose (2) abuse (3) and bruise (4) the crews (4) who choose (5) to use (6) my name wrong, they pay dues (7)"

The first time Kane did that it blew people's minds! In fact this became a Big Daddy Kane trademark. When done right it is a powerful punch. Years later Fabolous picked up where Kane and Kool Moe left:

"We've been (1) creeping (2) and sneaking (3) just to keep it (4) from leaking (5) We so deep in (6) our freaking (7) that we don't sleep on (8) the weekends (9)"

As shown here, there are many different and exciting techniques that emcees and rappers use in creative rhyming. This is the root of rapping. If an emcee thinks of a funny or relevant metaphor, he or she still has to create a rhyme to communicate it. The topics, the delivery of the rhymes, the image of the artist, all of that is secondary to being able to put words together in rhyme in the manner described.

RHYMECOLOGY EXERCISE:

Write a verse that rhymes the same word or rhyme scheme the entire time. This may be repeated as many times as possible, with four times being the minimum.

Use one, two or three syllables. Of principal importance is keeping the rhyme scheme flowing for the entire verse. If you only manage four lines in the same rhyme scheme, then add another four or eight from another rhyme scheme.

Once comfortable with this form, write a sixteen bar verse containing one rhyme scheme. Below is an example of dividing an eight bar verse into two easy rhyme schemes.

Example: *"Let's make sure we keep the rhyme flow*
for the entire verse as it will show
that you're a lyricist in the know
talent bubbling, about to blow,
That's why we keep typing
Hip-hop's our form of street fighting
Poetics of deep writing
For people to be reciting.

Those who flashin' don't blast, they still buffoons

Just blowin out hot air, they should fill balloons.

I'm like them shorties that could kill for goons

They started hustlin' in April to cop wheels in June.

- Elzhi, "Mt. Everest," The Keynote Speaker, 2013

The CHAIN-LINK RHYME Chapter

We have now begun to look into the complexities of hip-hop lyrics. Hip-hop has transformed itself numerous times over the years. It has gone through many stages, some good and some bad. (The song "Seasons" by the Cunninglynguists and Masta Ace documents the different stages of hip-hop through to today's form. While you are at it see the song "The Format" by the same artists). For those who have listened to hip-hop for twenty years or so, there are many things that compels us to return. There are many contemporary emcees at work who have taken the genre to a new level of originality.

We have looked at different rhyme patterns and shown you how how hip-hop can differ from other genres in that regard. We have looked at pioneering emcees and how they were ahead of their time with compound rhymes and multi-syllabic writing. This writing was fresh and new to the ear at that time. So what is the "next" level?

Even if you are dropping your compound rhymes in an a set pattern, this can become monotonous to the ear. In previous chapters I wrote about rhyme connection between the **set up** (first) and the **punchline** (second). Further, we added internal rhyme to fatten up the rhyme schemes. For example:

These chapters can be like brain (A) ink (B)

Feeding (C)on reading (C) about the chain (A)link(B)

There is no repentance(D) this time (E)

We are still ending the sentence (D) with rhyme (E)

The **end rhymes** (A&B) are at the end of the line and they don't make other appearances. The **internal rhyme** (C) appears in the second line but does not come back again. Let's now look at a four-line rhyme written by Louis Logic in the song "Misery Loves Comedy".

> *"That's the best way to treat disaster*
>
> *cuz if you let regret stay it eats you faster*
>
> *then your breastplate shakes*
>
> *when you breathe with asthma*
>
> *and death may take you to greener pastures."*

Louis Logic drops an obscene amount of multi syllabic and chain rhyme schemes on his album *Misery Loves Comedy*. This one stood out.

That's the best (A) way (B) to treat(C) disaster (D)

cuz if you let regret (A) stay (B) it eats(C) you faster (D)

then your breast (A) plate (B) shakes (B) when you breathe(C) w/ asthma (D)

and death (A) may (B) take (B) you to greener(C) pastures (D)

It is rare to rhyme this many syllables, in four consecutive lines, and all while telling a story. This man drops sixteen bars in no time and freestyles with the best of them. But when I interviewed Louis Logic he told me that sometimes it took him "months to write a song." Exactly my point. A lyricist SHOULD take time to write a song. To check his wordplay. To check his synonyms. To match his syllables. Louis Logic is writing songs and often stories. You can't do that in a few hours. Emcees write stories, rappers write bars.

Patterns like the Louis Logic one are super multi-syllabic but they are still just "matching". The rhyme pattern has 4 compound rhymes but besides for the **end rhymes**, nothing is connecting the different lines. The "next level" is called chain link rhyming, where your rhymes fall not only at the end of the line but also land sporadically throughout the verse. AZ is a master of this:

"Young and gifted,

my tongues prolific,

on a beach bungalows

how I brung in Christmas

with a street summer flow

from the hungriest district,

swiss kicks, crisp when I come to the picnics. "

In breaking this down you first notice "*Young and gifted*" rhyming with "*tongues prolific*". There are two different rhymes in those two lines.

Meaning, the word *"young"* would be classified as the (A) rhyme and *"gifted"* would be the (B). So the perfect match for those words comes in the next line of *"tongues"* and *"prolific"* with *"tongues"* being the (A) since it rhymes with young and *"prolific"* being the (B) since it rhymed with *"gifted"*.

In our AZ verse, he throws in a third line which does not match the (A) or (B) so the line of *"a beach bungalow"* becomes the (C) and (D). Then the emcee finishes the thought by another perfect rhyme with *"is how I brung in Christmas"*. *"Brung"* is linked to the (A) as was *"young"* and *"tongues"* and the word *"Christmas"* is a (B) rhyme to match the *"gifted"* and *"prolific"*.

> **Young and (A) gifted (B),**
> **my tongues (A) prolific (B),**
> **on a beach(C) bungalow is (D)**
> **how I brung in (A) Christmas (B)**
> **with a street(C) summer flow (D)**
> **from the hungriest (A) district (B),**
> **Swiss kicks, crisp (B) when I come to the (A) picnics (B)**

If the rhyme had ended with *"Christmas"* it would have been a great four bar rhyme. The (C) and (D) rhyme is the hanging line of *"beach bungalow"* which does not NEED to be rhymed with because AZ already ended the fourth line by matching *"Christmas"* with *"prolific"* and *"gifted"*. But AZ is no ordinary lyricist. He matches "beach bungalow" perfectly with *"street summer flow"* and then comes BACK to the A & B rhymes.

When he comes back to "*hungriest*"(A)and "*district*"(B) he has now made a chain link rhyme!

Notice how I have classified the word "*hungriest*" as a (A) rhyme. But what word does it rhyme with? Not "*tongue*", not "*young*" and not "*brung*" in all the other (A) rhymes. Nope, for this rhyme you have to look deeper. The one word, "*hungriest*", rhymes with the two and a half words of "*brung in Chris-*" from the line "*how I brung in Christmas*". Then to top it off he rhymes "*hungriest*" and "*brung in Chris-*" with "*come to the pic-*" from the line "*come to the picnic*".

This chapter has been a glimpse into the intricacies of hip-hop lyrics and what excites those who follow hip-hop. One could listen to hip-hop for a lifetime and never once notice the complexities of rhyme patterns but then one would be missing out on one of the most important facets to a hip-hop song.

Some Sick "Match Up" Lines:

I choose (A) to wallow (B) and I'll just swim (C) in my fat (D)

You refuse (A) to swallow (B) so I see ribs (C) from the back (D)

(Sage Francis)

Ripping (A)my cape (B) on the ground (C) that it dragged (D) on (E)
Tripping (A) on fate (B) hearing the sounds (C)of a sad (D) song (E)

(Sage Francis)

I abandoned (A) the mission (B) for recognition (C) & hype (D) bills (E)

By planning (A) and wishing (B) for simple vision (C) and life (D) skills (E)

 (J.Walker)

BONUS BIT: Study Kool G. Rap. Below is sample from "Fast Life".

Can you label the rhymes in this verse? What are the A's, B's, C's and so on. Where are the internals? When does it become a chain link?

Three _major players_ gettin _papers_ by the _layers_
And those that _portray us_ on the _block_ get _rocked_ like _Amadeus_
Fakers get used to shootin _targets,_ soon as the _dark hits_
Front on the drug _market,_ bodies get rolled up in a _carpet_
Those that _cheat us_ try to _beat us_ we got hookers with _heaters_
that'll stray pop and put more shells in your top than _Adidas_
Da _leaders,_ lookin straight _grimy_ in our Giorgio _Armani's_
You wanna _harm me_ &Nas you gotta get through a whole _army_
The ceelo _rollers_ money _folders_ sippin _bola_ holdin mad _payola_
Slangin Coke without the _Cola_
Me and _black_ don't fake _jacks_ but we might _sling one_
It ain't no _shame_ in our _game_ we do our _thing son_

DOUBLE BONUS: Extremely multi-syllabic, chain link albums

Louis Logic- *Misery Loves Comedy*

Sage Francis- *Personal Journals*

AZ- *Doe or Die/Legendary*

Big Pun- *Capital Punishment*

Eminem- *Infinite/Recovery*

Cam'ron-*Purple Haze*

MF Doom- *Danger Doom/Madvillany*

Papoose- *I'm Like That*

Elzhi- *Elmatic, Lead Poison*

Kool G. Rap- *4,5,6*

<u>RHYMECOLOGY EXERCISE</u>:

Match Rhyme.

1) Write two sentences that consist of four words (at least) from one sentence rhyming with four words from the next. Don't write ten words in one sentence and five in the next just to get the words aligned. The syllables should be similar too. For this exercise, the sentences don't need to make perfect sense. Stay focus on matching up the words in a similar fashion, and rhyming scheme to those shared in this chapter.

Chain Link Rhyme

2) Studying the examples and explanations in this chapter, create a chain link verse. Remember this is where you will be connecting rhyme schemes from the start to the end of your chosen pattern.

"With multisyllable rhyming, it's not like your just rhyming *might* and *fight*. You're rhyming *random luck* and *handsome fuck* with *we cop vans and trucks*- it ain't just doing the basics, because that's not ear catching."

- Kool G. Rap

The ELZHI & EMINEM Chapter

There are rapper, emcees and writers. There are great lyricists. Then there are Elzhi and Eminem. Both writers are Detroit natives who take rhyme patterns to new levels. Elzhi (known from Slum Village) is known for his complicated rhyme schemes, many of which contain multi-syllabic patterns, internal rhymes and alliteration, evocative imagery, simile and metaphor.

> *Yo, the day that hell snowed is when El fold,*
> *Poetry well told*
> *It's entertainin, keep niggaz trainin like the railroad*
> *Stingman, what I bring in is dope as the kingpen*
> *Slingin, OG's threw me beneath the wingspan*
> *Expert, through the less dirt, but still my tech squirt*
> *Bucked then, it gets tucked in, just like a dress shirt*

Every single rhyme is a compound one, often combining more than one word. *Hell snowed/El Fold/well told/raildroad* is all dropped within the first two lines and then *entertainin/trainin* is the internal rhyme in those same lines. He also uses wordplay in his simile when "*trainin like the railroad*", being that trains travel on railroads.

This also references working out physically.

A simile to start the second line, where what he *brings in is dope as the kingpen*, meaning that his rhymes are literally as good (dope) as materials bought and sold by the most reputable drug dealers (Note he is not boasting of selling drugs himself).

He is an *expert through less dirt* (meaning he gained high praise without going through the regular tribulations that most have to) but *still my tec squirt* (again three compound rhymes in one line) proving he is still of the streets and that when his tec does squirt, its *bucked then it gets tucked in* (perfect internal rhymes) *like a dress shirt.* He brings back the original rhyme scheme with a creative and crafty metaphor.. Another example:

**"I end careers, years/ pierce ears/
fierce with spears they say I'm gifted/
get lifted like the beers in Cheers!"**

Elzhi follows a rhyme pattern of his predecessor, Big Daddy Kane (multiple consecutive rhyming words), but adds an internal rhyme *gifted/lifted* which turns into a simile with a pop culture reference, *lifted like the beers in Cheers.* These subtle differences are consistent with taking an earlier rhyme scheme and then adding to it.

When one speaks of the evolution of rhyming, it is impossible not to mention the man Rakim called the "the Muhammad Ali" of rap, Marshall Mathers, aka Eminem. As he gained notoriety as a battle rapper in the mid 1990s when he was already dropping compound and internal rhymes packed with punchlines. Even though he was freestyle battling, his talent to put together complex rhyme schemes put him on the map, as seen here:

I've got so many ways to diss you/
that I'm playful with you/I'll let a razor slit you/
'till they staple stich you/everyone in this place will miss you/
if you try to turn my facial tissue to a racial issue.

Notice that the compound rhyme here is four syllables *ways to diss you/playful with you/razor slit you* etc. 7 perfect compound rhymes in essentially two lines that finish with knockout punchline "*try to turn my facial tissue to a racial issue*". From the "ways" until "ra" in "racial" he sticks with the "A" sound to begin his compound rhyme.

He brought together Rakim's compound rhymes and Kane's smashing of rhymes together and Lord Finesse type punchlines. Eminem baffled listeners with the constant onslaught of creative rhymes, which often had never been heard before. Whether battling or on his stunningly lyrical underground release "Infinite" or on his major label effort "Guilty Conscious", Eminem proved himself over and over again to be a technical mastermind of rhymes.

I let the beat commence/so can beat the sense/
of your elite defense/ I got some meat to mince-
a crew to stomp and two feet to rinse

Tell her you need a place to stay/you'll be safe for days/

if you shave your legs with Renee's razor blades

-"Guilty Conscience"

Another technique which Eminem has added to his repertoire is spreading assonance throughout a verses. With "Lose Yourself," Eminem essentially "bends" his words into a fitting rhyme scheme. Here's an example in where he intercuts two sets of vowel sounds together (lyrics bolded to indicate the long "o" rhyme and italicized to indicate the short "a" rhyme):

Oh, there **goes** *Rabbit,* he **choked**

He's **so** *mad,* but he **won't** give up *that easy,* **no**

He **won't** *have* it, he **knows** his **whole** *back's* to these **ropes**

It **don't** *matter,* he's **dope**

He **knows** *that,* but he's **broke**

He's **so** *stag*nant *that* he **knows**

When he **goes** *back* to his **mo**bile **home,**

That's when it's *back* to the *lab* again **yo**

Over the years many have deified Eminem as an emcee while others have claimed that he has been over hyped because of his skin color. Whatever the opinion is on his voice, his message, his albums or his legacy, when it comes to consistent rhyme schemes and the technical craft of lyric writing, there is no doubt that he rests very high on the list of all-time greats. In previous examples he smashed together numerous similar sounding compound rhymes into two lines, while on "Stimulate" he has four different rhyme schemes being spread across two lines:

Like a flame(A) in the night(B), like a ghost(C) in the dark(D)
There's a ray(A), there's a light(B), there's a hope(C), there's a spark(D)

Quick, how many things can you think of that rhyme with "If the shoe fits I'll wear it"? No not just "It" and not just "wear it". The entire phrase "If the shoe (A) fits (B) I'll wear (C) it (D)".

Well, if you are good you can find a few perfect rhymes for that phrase. Well, possibly just to prove a point, Eminem rhymed an entire verse with that phrase on the only guest appearance on Jay-Z's *The Blueprint*. Mostly they are perfect rhymes and a few times he has to bend some words to make them sound like perfect rhymes. The combination makes for one of the all-time greatest compound rhyme verses we have laid ears on. Now lay your eyes on it.

Since I'm in a position to talk to these kids and they listen

I ain't no politician but I'll kick it with them a minute

Cause see, they call me a menace and <u>if the shoe fits I'll wear it</u>

But if it don't, then ya'll swallow the <u>truth grin and bear it</u>

Now who's the king of these rude <u>ludicrous lucrative lyrics?</u>

Who could inherit the title, put the <u>youth in hysterics?</u>

<u>Using his music to steer it</u> sharing <u>his views and his merits</u>

But there's a <u>huge interference</u>,

they're saying, "<u>You shouldn't hear it.</u>"

Maybe it's hatred I spew, maybe it's <u>food for the spirit</u>

Maybe it's beautiful music I made for <u>you to just cherish</u>

But I'm debated, disputed, hated and <u>viewed in America</u>

as a motherfucking drug addict like <u>you didn't experiment?</u>

Now now, that's when you start to stare at <u>who's in the mirror</u>

and see yourself as a kid again, and <u>you get embarrassed</u>

And I got nothing to do but make <u>you look stupid as parents</u>

You fucking do-gooders –

*too bad you couldn't <u>**DO-GOOD** at marriage</u>!*

And do you have any <u>clue what I had to do</u> to get here I don't

think <u>you do so stay tuned</u> and keep your ears <u>glued to the stereo</u>

Cause here we go, he's {Jigga durra Jigga da chk Jigga}

And I'm the sinister, Mr. Kiss-My-Ass it's just the…

My count shows 18 rhymes with the phrase "If the shoe fits I'll wear it". This man is rhyming "huge interference" with "views and his merits" with "you shouldn't hear it" with "youth in hysterics" with "lucrative lyrics" and so on. The syllables match perfectly. All the way through.

Just sayin'.

EMIN∃M

If you had, one shot,
or one opportunity,
to seize everything you ever wanted,
one moment
Would you capture it?

*This thing called rhymin' is no
different than coal minin';
We both on assignment to
unearth the diamond.*

- Mos Def, "Travellin' Man," from DJ Honda's HII, 1998

The LYRIC WRITING EXERCISES Chapter

We often think about what we are used to hearing, seeing and feeling. This becomes what we are comfortable thinking about. And discussing. And then we write what we are comfortable discussing. And then after that, when we really have to think of a song concept, we write about what we think we are comfortable sharing.

Hip-hop artists often focus on the struggle that they have gone through, how much money they supposedly have, how they score with the opposite sex, their vices and basically how tight they are. Right? These are the staple themes of hip-hop. They are focal and predominant because hip-hop legends made them staples.

And that is exactly why it's imperative to develop the skills and hone your ability to branch out of the box of standard hip-hop topics. Notice that I write "the ability" to branch out because most hip-hop fans still want to hear some of those staple topics on their recently purchased rap albums. We still want to hear those punch lines, those creative metaphors and those references to the struggle. However, you are running a risk

> *It's imperative to develop the skills to branch out of the box of standard hip-hop lyrics.*

because those topics have been covered a million times by the legends. Most of us would prefer to hear Jay-Z talk about how he hustled his way to a record contract than an unknown emcee. *But here is the kicker.* Someone on a Jay-Z or Snoop Dogg level is more **confined to the topics** that they can write about than a new artist would be.

So this is something that new artists can use to their advantage. For example, a Lupe Fiasco might not have gained commercial success if he was simply rapping about the staple hip-hop topics. Lupe's first major commercial single was called "Kick, Push" a song about skateboarding! His talent and originality landed him a Grammy nomination.

Whether or not up and coming writers choose to use original topics is strictly up to that artist. However, in my opinion, it is key that they at least have the talent to do it when needed. So, the question is, how do you get to that level?

In my lyric writing workshops I often give topics to aspiring lyricists that force them to use terms and diction that may be out of their normal range. For example, at one workshops I might ask lyricists to finish the sentence, "A spaceship pulled up next to my car," or "I woke up inside of the refrigerator," or "The scrambled eggs were inside of my ears because… "

Normally what happens is some of the students write a very lyrical verse but after two lines they are off the topic and back onto their own agenda. Other students stay on the topic but won't have the rhyming patterns. It is a great way to learn where everyone is in their writing/rhyming skills.

Rap lyrics don't always have to be about staple topics to gain respect but they do have to rhyme well and they need to be creative. One of the most beautiful and inclusive aspects of hip-hop is that an artist may write a song about any topic and make it sound good.

- o Lupe Fiasco has a Grammy nominated song about two people who share a passion for skateboarding
- o Killah Priest has as song about teleporting across the earth and witnessing ancient civilizations.
- o Beastie Boys have a song about throwing eggs at people
- o Nas has a song which he tells...backwards

The list goes on and on and on. What these emcees have in common is the ability to write and rhyme on anything and that is what they do. A country singer would be laughed off of the stage if he were singing about a giant robot or teleportation. We have the leeway to write about anything in hip-hop. Take advantage of that freedom.

RHYMECOLOGY EXERCISE

Write a sixteen bar verse that starts with the line

"A spaceship pulled up next to my car…"

<u>Please check out these creative hip-hop songs</u>

"Alphabet Soup"- Masta Ace

"Rewind"- Nas

"I Gave You Power"- Nas

"I Used to Love H.E.R."- Common

"The Cool"- :Lupe Fiasco

"Sing About Me"- Kendrick Lamar

"Labels"- GZA

"Fame"- GZA

"Mathematics"- Mos Def

"Ebonics"- Big L

"Stan"- Eminem

"Heavy Mental"- Killah Priest

"A's & E's" Masta Ace & Ed O.G.

"Colors"- Elzhi

The OUTSIDE THE HIP-HOP BOX Chapter

Hip-hop is now in every household in the world. The novelty has worn off and people are craving the "new thing". Hip-hop has the ability to shift in many directions and the key for the next generation of writers to think outside the box.

Speaking of outside the box, one of the ways I gained some notoriety was through an AM radio sports talk show in Los Angeles. I noticed that "The Loose Cannons" show had a relatively free flowing energy in the show and is hosted by three cool guys, Steve Hartman, Mychal Thompson (of the 1980s Lakers) and Vic "Da Brick" Jacobs. One day, I heard that they were broadcasting from Hooters in Santa Monica. I shot down to Hooters to observe the show first hand. I decided to write a verse about what they were talking about that day. All of the lines were compound rhymes and based on *their* ideas and names. Lines like:

> *"Mychal, Randy Moss is skilled, yeah very nice*
> *But don't ever compare him to Jerry Rice.*
> *He won't even make the pro bowl this year, no way*
> *While Rice is known for making the cut, like O.J.*
> *Steve, I agree that playing the harmonica is hard,*
> *Like finding parking on Santa Monica Boulevard…"*

I went up to the producer of the show and read him what I had written. He told me to approach Mychal Thompson, who I had grown up watching on the Lakers in the 80's and read it to him. Within a few minutes, Steve Hartman handed me his own headset and I dropped my first sports verse live on the air to millions of listeners.

The scene could not have been any less hip-hop. There was no beat. I was in Santa Monica. At Hooters. However, thanks to hip-hop I was able to step into the restaurant, survey the scene, and create an on-the-spot verse. What I noticed was that people love to hear:

1) Their names

2) To know that this was a spontaneous work

So when I was mentioned to Mychal that Randy Moss was "very nice", his ears perked up as I was quoting him. And then I stamped the line with a bit of boldness by telling him not to "compare him to Jerry Rice". This shows it was in the moment, as they had just discussed it. And notice the importance of the word "very". If I had said "Moss is quite nice" that would not have been a perfect rhyme with "Jerry Rice". The word "very" was crucial.

A good lyricist can use his/her talent to make people relate in any situation. This is where all of the chapters and exercises come into play. To create a verse on the spot, about the people and or objects in the room, you have to be quick and creative and must be able to rhyme! To go from point zero to that stage, it takes active listening, multi-syllabic practice, and lyrical exercises, but it can be done if you are passionate about it and work hard at developing your skills.

RHYMECOLOGY EXERCISE:

Look at your surroundings and pick out something that has never been the subject of a verse. Maybe the furniture in the living room? Maybe create a verse including all the book titles on your shelf. Maybe open the cupboard or fridge and write a story including all the food you see. Maybe it is rhyming with all the countries you can pronounce on you're the globe?

The key is to create lots of possible rhymes and to stick with that topic. You may never use this verse but it is a fantastic way to sharpen your skills.

PERSISTENTLY PRACTICE YOUR PASSION!!

The FREESTYLE SECRETS Chapter

Full disclosure, I am not a great freestyler. I have dropped a gem or two in the past but it is not a focus for me anymore. I have found that I get more inspiration from creating concept songs or albums. The irony is that no matter how great your rehearsed songs are, no matter what complex your preconceived and written rhyme schemes you devise, no matter how many people you inspire, <u>a good freestyle will always impress more people.</u>

Freestyling is creative. Freestyling is a test. Freestyling is art.
Freestyling is hip-hop.

Freestyle is an improvisational form of rapping, performed with few or no previously composed lyrics, which is said to reflect a direct mapping of the mental state and performing situation of the artist. Usually the emcee is rapping about his immediate surroundings, people in the room, places or things which are within eye sight.

The affect that an unscripted, witty and real freestyle has on a crowd can far supersede any written song. When the a listener hears their name thrown into an impromptu verse, when they hear the name of the club in which they are standing or see an artist rhyming about things which they see on stage, the listener goes from just a spectator to part of the show! And that is a special feeling.

During a set I often perform deep, intricate and meaningful lyrics. I also almost always drop a random meaningless freestyle towards the end of my set. Which one do you think causes the audience to come up to after the show? You got it. The freestyle!

While freestyling is off the top of the head, there are certain secrets which you can use to get the audience in the palm of your hand.

<u>Helpful Hints(Big 5)</u>

1) Let the audience know that you are freestyling! Take a person in the audience and plug in his or her name in the beginning of your freestyle.

   "I know you are used to hearing rappers flow songs/ but ask Greg I am just going to make it up as I go along".

2) Have line for the venue that you performing in.

   "This is the part of the night in which I start flowing/ and want to thank you all for coming out to Genghis Cohen".

3) Be ready to talk about what you are wearing. Point out the article of clothing as you mention it.

This is a freestyle not some mean rap/ you know I had to come through in my green hat/ I couldn't rock anything that's blue/ cuz then I wouldn't be matching my shoes!"

4) Claim something specific to the night.

"I'm magical, they call me a rhyming wizard/ I can perform on stage or outside in that blizzard!"

5) Call out someone or something in the crowd and point to it.

"Rhymes like these might leave you in shock/ Like the reflection from this dudes watch!"

I have seen many people freestyle better than they write. In a way it is unfortunate because freestyling doesn't get you paid. It earns you instant respect, but well written, original songs are the key to getting paid. If you are not a great freestyler but feel like you need to add this skill to your repertoire, these 5 ideas will help. You may not master all five but you should include a few of them.

It is advisable to have an idea of which of those five you are going to use before you start to freestyle. These are the lines that are going to stand out. These are the lines that will blow people's minds.

Just as important however, is the knowledge that you have to be able to fill the lines in-between the big five. Everyone has different "fill-in" lines that they can go to without thinking. This is the line that you can spit while thinking about what you might say next. I usually say something like, "Yeah I look in the crowd and I see smiles/ so I know they love my freestyle" or I say "I'm rocking insane/Coming through off the top of the brain." Because I can say those lines without thinking, I can free my brain to think of the BIG **5**.

Suggestions for the Fill in lines:

YOUR NAME/RESIDENCE/OR A MESSAGE YOU BELIEVE IN

The ART OF STORYTELLING Chapter

In the previous chapters we primarily worked on single subject verses to hone our rhyme skills. This next exercise utilizes a combination of random topics and subjects to create a story.

Story telling is nothing new in hip-hop. The one of the early major releases in such a manner was done by the legend Slick Rick(who had an album appropriately titled *The Art Of Storytelling*). Many other artists have dedicated a track or two to a story for example Nas ("Shootouts" on *It was Written*), Masta Ace ("A Block Episode" on *Disposable Arts*), Notorious B.I.G. ("I Got a Story to Tell" on *Life After Death*) and many more.

One of the more challenging exercises that I give students is what I call the Super Size Combo (seemed like a good name sometime down the line). I decide on an animal, a toy, a person, food item, a car, something in the environment, and then a random item, and write all of them on a board in front of the class. I ask the students to create a verse that incorporates each one of the subjects. That is the only rule of this exercise: Every subject has to be used in the verse. For the more advanced lyricists I ask that they turn the verse into a story. For the beginners, a verse incorporating each subject is sufficient.

For example: Create a verse with; *a lion, an X-Box, a lake, George Bush, a burrito, a pacifier and a BMW*. This is exercise normally gets about

15 minutes during a workshop. The key is to get yourself out of your normal writing box and to do it under pressure. This is how those subjects may form a short verse.

"I didn't want George Bush to trouble you

So I went to the white house n put him in my BMW

And since politicians are classified liars

I had to shut him up with my son's pacifier

We started driving towards the lake

I told him we want presidents that strive to be great

And are not going to cheat folks,

By now we could smell Taco Bell and its burritos

I told George, no, none for you

and bought some food for my hungry crew

who were back at the pad playing X-Box

I wanted to wreck shop but the next stop

was the lake and thanks to fate

there was a starving lion in front of the gate

So without a mental pause

I let George out, covered in sauce..."

A good lyricist can use humor, politics, and pop culture references in a story. A good lyricist may use any number of these tactics as long they tie it together with their rhymes. Again, it all starts with the ability to rhyme and that is why we have taken time and chapters to practice basic, intermediate and multi-syllabic rhyming. Once that aspect develops into a strength, a skill and a habit, and you return to verses, you'll look forward to putting more syllables together. Instead of simply saying, "Politicians are liars", I throw in the word "classified" before "liars" just so that it rhymes better with "pacifiers".

Why do we do this? Sales are down note only because the internet and pirating, but also because creativity is lacking, in my opinion. That issue starts with top commercial artists and trickles down to those sitting in my lyric workshops. It is not that they don't have the skill to create original songs, but often it simply has not occurred to them. Rap is not going to disappear, but the **old staple topics of negativity are on their way out**! They have to be. In the near future the industry will be looking for innovative writers who have the wherewithal to create rhymes on the spot, about any subject.

CONCEPT ALBUMS

Not only are there creative concept songs in hip-hop out there, there are also entire concept albums where each song acts as a chapter in a book. What is fun about these albums is the lyrics within the song also are following along the lines of the stories. Top 5 lists are always debatable and there are dozens of good concept albums. But in my opinion there are three that stand out above the rest.

1) *Mickey MauSe* by Mickey Factz (2012)

    Mickey Factz literally changes his identity to Mickey MauSe, a 1980's graffiti artist who was kicked out of his house and had to go through the hardships of the era. Factz did tons research to properly represent the era, including interviews with Andy Warhol, samples from Hulk Hogan and more. What is mind blowing is that Mickey never raps as Mickey Factz, the entire album is rapped from the pseudo character Mause, who details to us what it was like to experience the 1980s in New York City as a graffiti artist. There are no references to modern hip-hop lingo, no featured artists and it is written and performed in present tense and done so well that it is hard to tell what year or era it was recorded it.

2) *A Prince Among Theives* by Prince Paul (1999)

This has been the standard bearer for hip-hop concept albums for many years. Written, produced, arranged and scored by Prince Paul in 1999, it is the story of an aspiring emcee named Tariq, who needs to gather up a bunch of money in a short amount of time in order to record a demo tape before a meeting with RZA of the Wu-Tang Clan. Desperate for money, Tariq turns to his friend the local drug dealer who gives makes him earn his keep. They encounter crooked police, arms dealers, ambushes, backstabbing and more. Each character is played by a legendary emcees such as Big Daddy Kane, Everlast, Chubb Rock, Kool Keith and more. Complete with skits, this is as close to a movie on record as you will EVER hear.

3) *Disposable Arts* by Masta Ace (2001)

Probably the most appreciated of the three albums, Disposable Arts has had a good run as my "favorite album". The concept follows a Brooklyn man's (played by Ace) release from prison, his return home, and his life at "The Institute of Disposable Arts".

Masta Ace injects his own story throughout the concept which makes it more personable and really connects you with the emcee. As Ace is walking out, the prison guards makes fun of his clothing to which Ace defends "1995, this was the shit". Not ironically, the last Masta Ace album came out in 1995. This implies that he has been in hip-hop jail since then. This is most likely because 1995-2001 was dominated by the "bling bling" era and Hype Williams videos were rappers are throwing money off of speedboats. His first lines show how he, a talented emcee, has been feeling during the during the whole era. "Its been five years at least, waiting for a piece, bouncing off these walls awaiting my release". The double meaning between his career and the character he is playing goes throughout the album.

He eventually enrolls in "The institute of Disposable Arts", which is a cheesy school which teaches him how to make beats and how to rap. The irony is again thick here as, in this album Ace redefined his delivery and in effect, learned how to rap again.

Each song is a chapter which leads into the next until the last two songs "Dear Diary" and "No Regrets" which are Ace at his humble and self-deprecating best.

This album is 15 years old as I write this and I am still feeling like I am getting to know it.

(P.S. If you get this album, like "get" it and "GET" it, then you will also love the prequel to the story "*A Long Hot Summer*", which is only one microscopic hair less impressive).

RHYMECOLOGY EXERCISE:

Write a verse with the following subjects.

Take more than 30 minutes, people.

1) A hamster, Legos, a mountain, Kobe Bryant, piece of salmon, a drill and a motorcycle.

2) A kangaroo, Gi-Joe action figure, Angelina Jolie, a watermelon, a jump rope and a Corvette.

10 Great Storytelling Songs

"A Perfect Circle"- Louis Logic

"Who Rotten 'Em"- Slick Rick

"Gold"- GZA

"8 Million Stories"- A Tribe Called Quest

"Loves Gonna Getcha"- Boogie Down Productions

"Stray Bullets"- Organized Konfusion

"Friend of Foe"- Jay-Z

"Dance with the Devil"- Immortal Technique

"Black Steel in the Hour of Chaos"- Public Enemy

"I Seen a Man Die"- Scarface

The (W)RAP UP Chapter

I'm not big on long goodbyes. Let's do a quick review with a few pointers and you are on your own.

You picked this book because you wanted to become a great writer in the hip-hop genre. This book does not teach you about breath control, about what beats to choose and how to ride them, about how to handle the mic on stage, or about what image is hottest selling right now. You can find your own niche and run with that. Images, beats, and styles all will come and go. They will evolve and revolve. What stays constant is the need for great written songs that challenge listeners to think and feel. But you are not going to get the respect in hip-hop unless your rhyming skills are sharp as a knife.

My parting suggestions follow:

1) Keep Everything You Write!

It doesn't matter if it is a two bar punch line or an entire album. If it is on a napkin or if it is a file on your computer. Keep them all together. Label each notebook or file (Ideas, Songs, Unfinished pieces, One Liners, etc). You never know when they will come in handy. Plus, it is fun to see how far you have come!

2) Write Concepts

There have been over thirty years of emcees and rappers telling us how great they are. Thirty years of random raps over looped beats. Which are the songs that have lasted through time. "The Message", "Summertime", "They Reminisce Over You", "Dear Mama". Songs written to a concept have a better chance of lasting through the generations.

3) Push Your Limits

Don't settle on rhymes. Don't be happy with "I'm writing till I get those profits/cuz I have made it when with convicts". Push it until its "Can't stop, till I'm achieving those profits/and its lamb chops, while eating with convicts.". Why rhyme two syllables a line when you can rhyme 5 words a line?

4) One Great Track

While you are going to be writing and writing and recording and recording, don't "put out" songs unless they are up to par. The game has changed since hip-hop has blown up and the internet has made it so easy to hear so many emcees. Before you put something out to the public, make it good. Make it a concept. Perfect your flow. Pick a great beat. Then promote the hell out of it. Don't give someone the opportunity to judge you on your old or weaker works. Create a great track and give it away free (just this one). The rest will follow.

And lastly. Remember this.

The hip-hop industry is wack. Hip-hop itself is beautiful.

Your craft is a lifelong process that will evolve as long as you want it to. Your dedication to expanding and improving your rhyme schemes and lyrics is a journey that you will always be grateful you took.

Keep Writing.

The DANTE ½ Chapter

I would be kick myself if I failed to mention Dante Alighieri and the rhyme scheme he CREATED in the early 1300's. You read that right, 1300's. Dante has been called "the Father of the Italian language".[2] In Italy, Dante is often referred to as il Sommo Poeta ("the Supreme Poet") and il Poeta.

Dante wrote the The Divine Comedy (many just call it Dante's Inferno) in a language he called "Italian", a sort of combination literary language mostly based on the regional dialect of Tuscany, but with some elements of Latin (most poets wrote in Latin only at the time) and other regional dialects. He deliberately aimed to reach a readership throughout Italy including laymen, clergymen and other poets. Meaning, it was high art yet street at the same time. By creating a poem of epic structure (100 chapter poem!) and philosophic purpose (calling out Catholics Popes and sinners), he established that the Italian language was suitable for the highest sort of expression.

The name Dante is still relevant because he wrote one of, if not THE, greatest pieces of literary art mankind has ever known.

And he did so in perfectly crafted iambic pentameter rhyme.

PATTERN Terza Rima

Nel mezzo del cammin di nostra vita (a)

mi ritrovai per una selva oscura (b)

ché la diritta via era smarrita. (a)

Ahi quanto a dir qual era è cosa dura (b)

esta selva selvaggia e aspra e forte (c)

che nel pensier rinova la paura! (b)

Tant'è amara che poco è più morte; (c)

ma per trattar del ben ch'i' vi trovai, (d)

dirò de l'altre cose ch'i' v'ho scorte. (c)

Io non so ben ridir com'i' v'intrai, (d)

tant'era pien di sonno a quel punto (e)

che la verace via abbandonai. (d)

Terza rima is a three-line stanza using chain rhyme in the pattern.

A/B/A/ B/C/B/C/D/C/ D/E/D

Dante used that exact rhyme scheme for 14,233 lines over 100 chapters (or Cantos in Italian) to describe his journey through hell, purgatory and paradise. The great writer T.S. Elliot said that "Dante and Shakespeare divide the world, there is no third".

I write about him only to remind you that there was life and there were poets and lyricists long before, and there will be long after hip-hop.

To see how this feels in English I added Shelley's *Ode to the West Wind* with a couplet ending:

O wild West Wind, thou breath of Autumn's being, (a)

Thou, from whose unseen presence the leaves dead (b)

Are driven, like ghosts from an enchanter fleeing, (a)

Yellow, and black, and pale, and hectic red, (b)

Pestilence-stricken multitudes: O thou, (c)

Who chariotest to their dark wintery bed (b)

The winged seeds, where they lie cold and low, (c)

Each like a corpse within its grave, until (d)

Thine azure sister of the Spring shall blow (c)

Her clarion o'er the dreaming earth, and fill (d)

(Driving sweet buds like flocks to feed in air) (e)

With living hues and odours plain and hill: (d)

Wild Spirit, which art moving everywhere; (e)

Destroyer and preserver; hear, oh, hear! (e)

Following this ½ chapter, I include a piece, which I challenged myself to write in Terza Rima.

The Story of Charlie and Lashell

Jeffrey T. Walker

(Meant to be read outloud)

There was a boy named Charlie

Who's teeth rarely showed

For him the smiles are hard, see

He's lacking the tools to grow

His parents have been divided

But not divorced, of course,

They're religious and confided

In the pastor that they have to force

Themselves to touch

And in private they scream until they're horse,

Charlie hears all this over his tunes

He looks for the remote control

So he can squeeze on the volume

Not knowing he has lost his soul,

He wants to go outside to play

But he doesn't get the chance

And he's not sure what to say

When asked about that ambulance

That came to his house

So he lies and says "Mom fell in a dance",

His teachers have suspicions

But can't get to the truth

So many Dads in prisons

They see how it affects the youth

And they want to believe in something

So they pick Charlie's family

Where there's a back there's a front and

They call on Charlie randomly,

To draw pictures of his happy home

so he can smile and stand in the

front of the class, straight faking,

"He's got lunch money" they notice

But his inside his body is aching

He knows his parent's marriage is hopeless

"Blonde hair, blue eyes, he's so cute"

Yeah that's what he always hears

But he feels rotten at the root

So he tugs on his ears

Teachers look the other way

Never noticing his hidden tears,

There is a girl who sits by him

Her name is Lashell

She has a deep cut on her shin

A scar from the time when she fell

She was jumping robe with her friends

Just laughing in the sunshine

She said "Watch this Jenn"

Before she tripped on the rope, the one time

She didn't wear her knee pads

She bled like the victim of some crime,

Her friends didn't know what to do

So they ran up to the nearest car

It was an officer dressed in blue

About ready to hit the bar

He wasn't in the mood for this

No not on this day

He was feeling rude and pissed

Because he didn't get his overtime pay

So he took a deep breath

Looked at the girls and straight walked away,

Lashell's parents were doctors

Oh yes they were

Took her to the park to play soccer

And invested in her

But this day they were gone

Working a medical convention

They left their numbers on

The fridge in case she needed attention

But she used the paper for tic-tac-toe

So she was embarrassed when she was let in

To class where she sat in the back

She had good grades

And could recite all the facts

But stayed away from all "A's"

Because her friends couldn't keep up,

She sat next to Terrell

Who was known to erupt

"Umm, are you OK Lashell??"

She looked past the teacher

And told her she fell,

The blood was still red

Stuck to her brown skin

Teacher shaking her head

Looking down at her skin

"Isn't there something you want to say?"

"Uh, no I can't say that there is"

"Well, go to the office and stay"

I think someone's beating their kid

Is what the teacher thought, not

Knowing that she hid

All of her assumptions under her glasses

She thought she was protecting Lashell

By removing her from classes

But she really put her through hell

Her parents went from meeting to meeting

With threats of foster homes

And accusations of beatings

Lashell and Charlie,

Well, now their grown

Not knowing their teachers views

Became their own.

Jeffrey T. Walker
2016

RHYMECOLOGY

The Rhymecologist can be reached at:

rhymecology@gmail.com

www.rhymecology.com

www.facebook.com/rhymecology

Notes

Notes

Notes

Notes

Notes

Notes

Notes

19249386R00081

Printed in Great Britain
by Amazon